DUETS FOR FLUTE & GUITAR

Volume 2

Giuliani • Faure • Ibert
• Villa-Lobos • Schubert

Grand Sonata Op.85

3 taps (3/4 measure) precede music.

Allegro maestoso

I.

Mauro Giuliani

3

II.

4 taps (1 1/3 measures) precede music.

Andante molto sostenuto

4

5 taps (1 2/3 measures) precede music.

III.

Scherzo

5

6

Scherzo D.C.

2 taps (1 measure) precede music.

IV.

Allegretto espressivo

7

9

Sicilienne

Gabriel Fauré

Entr'Acte

Jacques Ibert

6 taps (2 measures) precede music.

Allegro vivo

14

riten

PP

tr

sff

5 taps (1 measure) precede music.

Distribuçào De Flôres

2 taps precede music

Villa-Lobos

20

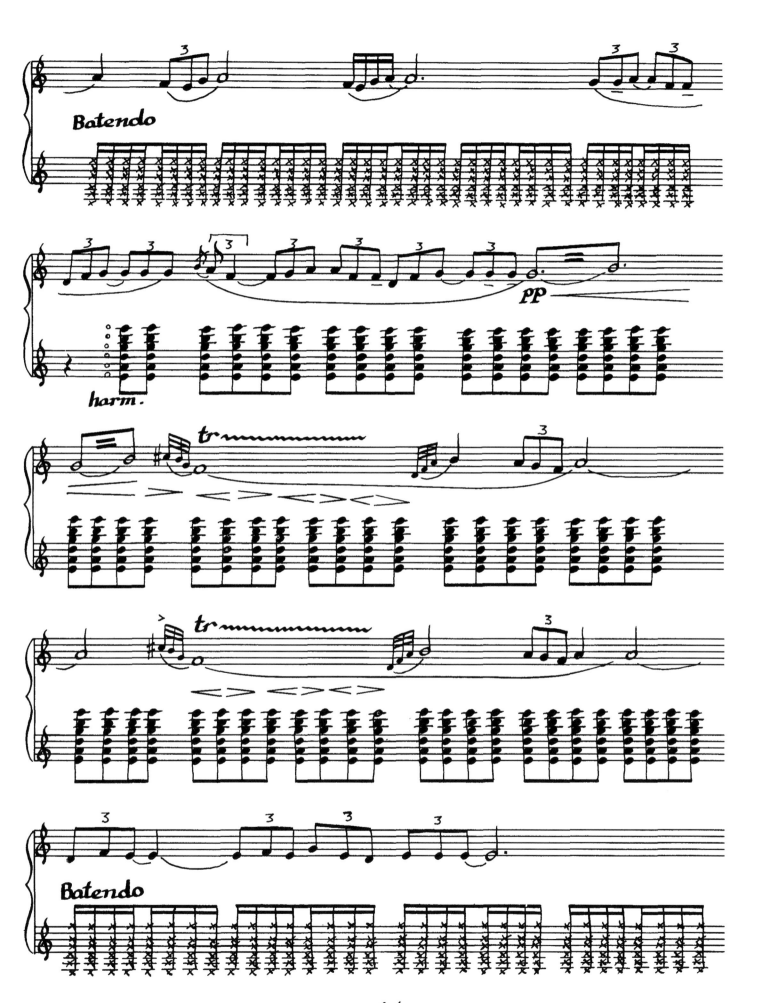

Batendo

harm.

Batendo

21

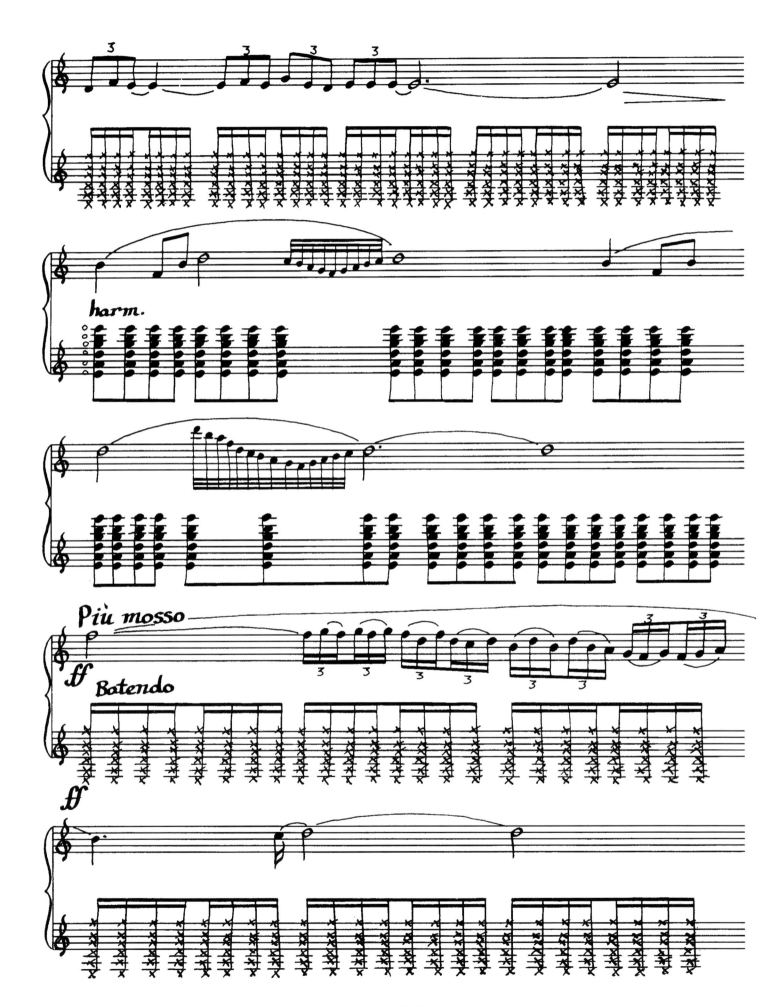

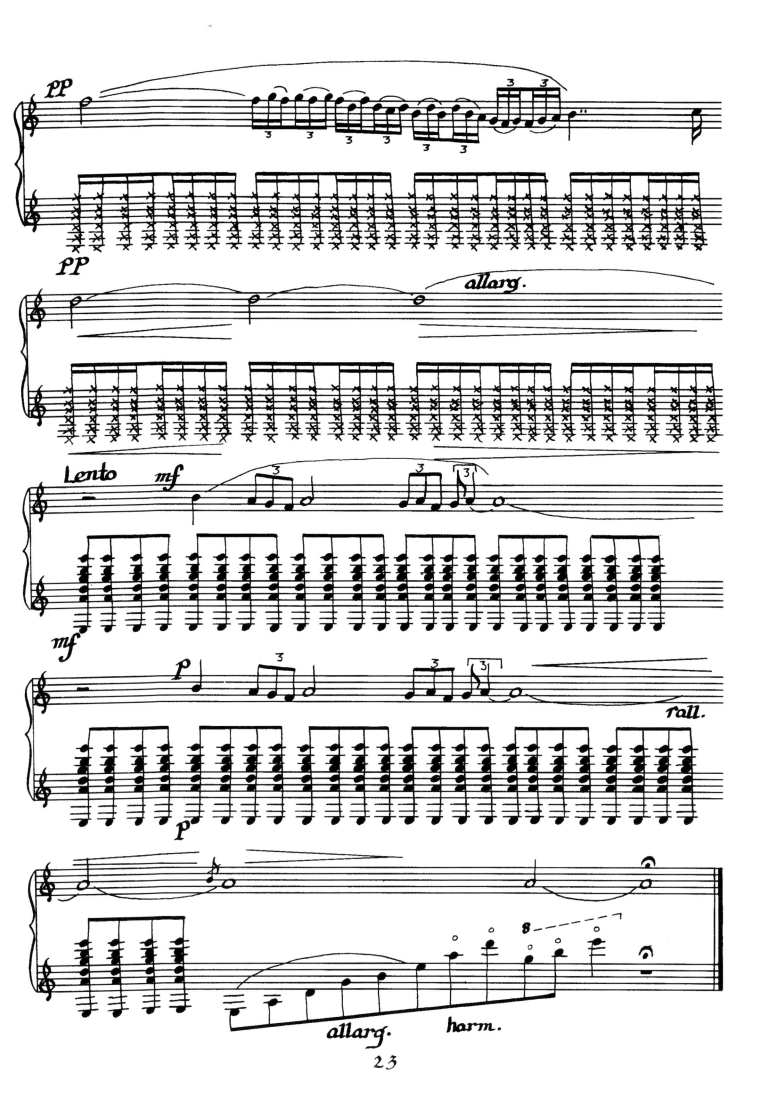

An Die Musik

Franz Schubert

2 taps (½ measure) precede music.